Treading The Helix

Stephen Beattie

*To Liz, I hope you
enjoy the poems,
with best wishes from
Stephen.*

Indigo Dreams Publishing

First Edition: Treading The Helix

First published in Great Britain in 2011 by:
Indigo Dreams Publishing
132 Hinckley Road
Stoney Stanton
Leics
LE9 4LN

www.indigodreams.co.uk

ISBN 978-1-907401-35-0

British Library Cataloguing in Publication Data. A CIP record for this book can be obtained from the British Library.

Designed and typeset in Palatino Linotype by Indigo Dreams.

Cover design by Ronnie Goodyer at Indigo Dreams.

Printed and bound in Great Britain by Imprint Academic, Exeter.

Papers used by Indigo Dreams are recyclable products made from wood grown in sustainable forests following the guidance of the Forest Stewardship Council.

For
Kimberley, Laura, Melissa and Sophie.

Acknowledgements

A heartfelt thank you to Alison Chisholm for teaching me the craft of poetry and putting up with my misplaced apostrophes. I would also like to thank all the members of the Thursday poetry class and Southport Writers' Circle for their support and encouragement. To Harvinder for the inspiration and lastly thank you Ronnie and Dawn for giving me this opportunity.

Pipedreams, 1st prize Pennine Ink competition 2009.

The Taste Of Apples, 1st prize Kings Lyn Writers' Circle poetry competition 2007.

A First Christmas, previously published in Writelink Christmas Ezine 2009.

Can Stones Ever Love and *Curtain Call*, previously published in Farrindon Arts competition anthology 2008.

The Other Side Of The Sky, 2nd prize Fylde Brighter Writers poetry competition 2009.

The End Of The Pier previously published in Literal Translations (USA).

An Elephant In The Bloom, 1st prize Writing Magazine 'Robert Burns' competition 2009, published in Writing Magazine.

I'll Call You, 2nd Prize Writers' News last line competition 2009, published in Writers' News.

Fireworks In The Park and *We Do Like* previously published in Ormskirk Writers' Circle North West Writers Anthology 2009.

A Wasps Nest, previously published in A Pride Of Lines' anthology by Driftwood Press 2006.

Contents

Treading The Helix

Then

Winter's east wind paints
fen and wold in stark purity.
Powdery drifts fold lintel high,
trapping sound,
curving words into forgotten corners.

The world pauses,
farmyard a monochrome island
throwing out crags of house, barn and haystack.

We children help rescue udder swollen cattle,
pilot them through pearlescent fields
to the dairy where their milk is drained
into grey galvanized churns
that are left uncollected in the lane.

Our wet-mittened hands sculpt statues,
smooth and shape contours,
define features with carrot and coal.

That night we peer from the bedroom window
willing our misshapen creations to move,
only to watch them fade in the thaw
that arrives faster than the storm.

Life returns to the long sigh of February,
the milk is collected, lambs are born
and the tedious mud of the garden
is dotted with black and orange memories.

Pipedreams

I remember being seven
and sitting with grandfather.
Farming days were long over
but his nature still tied him
to the ritual of seasons
and his ever present pipe.

The briar bowl was constantly stoked
with thin strips of tobacco,
shredded and bedded down
with toil-grained finger and thumb.
Hands would cup against an imaginary breeze
as the Swan Vesta was sandpaper scraped.
With an draw of breath the scented
pyre would be furnaced, spent match
dispatched to the ash-tray where it latticed
with countless others. Then came the slow motion
cirrus of blue smoke weaving around the room.

In the nursing home
they took his pipe away,
he said he didn't miss it
(in those days it didn't do to complain)
but his right hand still
cradled the absent talisman.

Sunday Afternoon 1967

Cerise peaks of Angel Delight
stand to attention in stainless steel
dessert dishes. Mine is achingly close,
forbidden until the last curl
of egg and cress is consumed.

I anticipate the sprinkle of hundreds
and thousands; watch their colours seep
into soft edged rainbows.

We're ordered to eat slowly with a teaspoon,
our budget doesn't run to large portions,
I can't help myself and it disappears
in a staccato of metal on metal.

I slyly lick the bowl, forgetting
that mothers are all seeing;
the single second helping goes to my sister.
I vow to hide her favourite doll.

Soul Searching

I'm nine years old
surrounded by the damp walls
of the Congregational chapel.

The dour pine pulpit
wears a rainbow skirt of books.
It's prize-giving,
a reward for enduring
another year of Sunday school.

I'm called forward,
my boy-fingers briefly clasp
Reverend Walker's mottled claw.
I return to my seat
(no pews, just plywood
and metal, good for the soul).

That night under a cliché
of blanket and torch
I read my trophy,
'The Concise History Of The World'.
By dawn I know of Darwin
and apes, of Popes
and protestants
and ancient rain forests.

But there's no mention
of a seven day plan,
or Eden, snakes
and forbidden fruit.

I resolve to ask the Reverend,
half aware I'll have to face
that little-big word;
faith.

Fusion

The black leaded grate anticipates
news print twists, slivered kindling
and the glow of anthracite,
freshly mined from the scuttle;
a physic to break the fever.

> A man sits cradling a stone maul
> flaking flints as ions cluster
> the atmosphere and beasts breathe
> sounds of approaching thunder.

Hands; caring hands
construct a weave of wood
paper and coal. A match
is sandpaper scratched; in a brief
second of sulphur the flame ignites

> the desiccated grasslands;
> and the stone bears down to accompanying
> stutters of dry lightening.
> The man sees; instantly tastes
> infinity, becomes shaman, savours
> the magic of burning flesh and fire

that now sends its first spires
stalagmiting up the chimney.
The pallid child draws heat,
watches the shaman lead his tribe
through the flames, hears the chant
as he slips below the warm quilt;
understanding.

The Taste Of Apples

They were cookers
rather than eaters.
Every autumn dad claimed
the crop; each emerald orb
was wrapped in yesterdays' news
then placed in scented hibernation
under the marital bed.

One year as winter clawed deep
they perfumed the room
masking the tartness of distance
that crept through the house.

By next harvest he'd left;
the apples slipped from my infant-school
fingers to lie amongst the windfalls,
bruised beyond use.

I tried to eat one. It had the bitter taste
of realization. I left it to rot.

Is Levi Strauss Truly God?

I won a prize at Sunday school
and with the proceeds purchased
my first pair of Levis'.
And being a cliché I sat in the bath
clad only in indigo denim,
hoping the cloth would close tight
around my adolescent legs.
They had twenty-eight inch flares;
the Levis' that is, not my legs.

Things started to happen;
I developed a liking for linen shirts,
shunned the barbers,
read translations from the Tibetan
Book Of The Dead,
everything could be explained
by saying it was 'Zen'.

Life has progressed and I've had many
gods since then;
but none has provided
me with the price of a pair of jeans.
Maybe there's something in it after all?

The One That Got Away

They said I did all I could,
anyone would have done the same,
I wasn't to blame myself.
When you're ten you want to believe
words like those.

When you're ten nightmares are real
but you don't expect them to cause
years of fear. Photographs fade
and sick-skinned newspaper cuttings crumble.
The images ingrained on your soul
lurk like lurid paintings
brush stroked in guilt.
As vivid as that day by the river.

In a midnight room I jolt awake.
There's the smell of bad water,
and the badness in me.
Furniture fragments, walls recede
revealing a reed stippled bank
sloping to water's edge.

In July heat we scavenge
for timid sticklebacks and minnow.
Tired and sun scorched,
our skins too young to sweat,
we bicker and bark
as question mark clouds cloak the horizon.

We reach the weir.
One of us suggests a dare.
The next thing I see is your broken body
turbid in the churn of flotsam.

I run. I run. And I run.

And when they ask me
I say we were scared
of the man in the overcoat
who was old enough to sweat.

Longfern Drive 1973

Older than me, ancient twenty something's
ensconced in a shambolic Victorian villa
just to the left of suburbia. Commune dwelling
degree holders chose to pack cardboard boxes
on the day shift. Peace love and tolerance
their mantra; the gas meter by-passed.

Their girlfriends had centre parted curls,
dressed in imitation Edwardian
courtesy of Laura Ashley. They assumed unlikely
elfin names, served dhal, Feta and Vin Rouge
on a pre fashionable pine table;
guests always had to pay.

Postprandial guitars were strummed for hours,
tunes seldom achieved. Governments
were brought to their knees with stoned rhetoric.
But nothing good lasts forever; these days the heroes
of my naivety arrange mortgages, extract teeth
or own companies that pack things in cardboard boxes.

Lip Service

Solstice has been banished
along with our gods
of stream, field and forest.
In the sacred place
where holly and mistletoe grew
alien men of the cloth
have built a temple to a new deity.
We are forced to worship
the three who are one,
we have to believe
in what we can't comprehend.
Brought to our knees
we are preached new rituals
in words of a foreign tongue;
heads bowed we recall older truth.

Outside our dead rot in earth
denied fire's cleansing
or goods for the journey.
But the yew tree still grows strong
and in the secret oak grove
a golden blade falls
as death is given
so we may regain light.

In Loving Memory...

I once stood tall and free
in a family of forest,
decked in leaf, lichen and life.

Now stripped of skin
my sapless flesh has become
plank and newel, pierced by nails
and turning screws.
I'm reduced to a geometry
created by man's hand,
given the name of someone who's now dust.

I'm exiled in this graveyard
surrounded by death yet still seeing,
able to watch my brothers and sisters
dance in the breeze, naked in winter,
reborn in each budburst of spring.

But those who take time to rest
on my slatted ribs
live and die only once;
they sit and reflect on love and loss.
Together we're imprisoned by memory.

New Delhi Street Scene

Standing outside the carpet shop,
clutching a durrie that maybe
once saw Kashmir, I wonder
why we tourists only talk about the cows,
how their milk comes from the mother goddess,
how their sanctity binds together
the chaos of the cosmos.

No one mentions the dogs;
jaundiced furred, amber-eyed
mongrels that litter the city
from suburb to centre.
Worshipped by none, not even
pitied by pale skinned Europeans.

Then, from around the corner,
a crippled beggar boy crabs
along the pavement,
his limbs impossibly twisted,
hands pleading for rupees.

In silent guilt we board the coach;
someone points to a sacred cow,
all eyes focus on it. Unseen
the beggar curls up against a sleeping dog;
the closest he'll ever come to the comfort
of another beating heart.

A Teardrop On The Face Of Eternity
(Taj Mahal)

Fingers of mist stroke the river's surface,
parakeets jewel dawn sky
and the ever-present incense
of India hangs in the air.

Hand in hand we stare in silence,
around us low whispers
of foreign tongues melt into a frisson.
But this is no tower of Babel.
This is the perfect symmetry of love
awakening, as it does each day,
to a blush of sunrise, a princess
caught in beauty's isolation.

We shed our shoes
feel the cool stone under our feet.
All distance has departed
this building has become
more than marble and mortar.

I think of miles travelled,
of the teardrop in your eye.
When we finally speak
we talk of love and rivers;
some now dry, or maybe waiting
for the flood of memory
that flows through inlaid knots
of carnelian, jasper and jade.

And us?
Are we intruders here
eavesdropping on the echo
of another's adoration?

It's time to go.
I kiss your lips
and then the stone;
we leave our mark.

A First Christmas

Long before the frost flecked dawn
she treads quietly down the stairs
feet as light as a butterfly's caress.
Clad in sari and overcoat
against this alien chill
she brews strong-spiced tea;
thinks of a village a world away,
of a boy, of a kiss that exiled her forever.

Today her aunts and cousins will celebrate
this foreign festival, give gifts
to their English friends;
feel that they belong,
that they are accepted.
Then when the guests have left
and the pretence is done,
talk will turn to her wedding
to the 'good kind man'
who for her only exists in a photograph.

She shivers and bows down
before the tinsel trimmed tree
that shrines the corner of the room
and prays that wise men will re-write her future.

Life Imitating Art

I'm sat at a café table
in the Tate, (modern of course),
surrounded by starving artists
masquerading as waiters,
their aprons hanging half mast,
an ironic post millennium statement;
or so I'm told.

I'm also given to understand
that Klimt's come to town
and the soup is off.
Well I don't know a lot about art
but I know what I like
and that would be some food, please.

On the far shore of this Bohemian tide
sits a man, his hair an inept wig maker's
vision of a mane. He throws his napkin
to the floor and roars,
'Gustav, I'm starved.'
I suspect he's the token poet.

Brief Encounter

The woman in the café
wears dark glasses;
it's November.
Small gems pepper the frames.
I decide she must be
pretentious or blind,
or just blindly pretentious.

I'm sitting two tables
and a lifetime away,
eking out a frothy coffee
filling day's emptiness.

Maybe she's continental?
I've never been abroad
but I believe that women
act differently there.

Maybe she's a spy?
Shading secrets
while wrestling with ciphers
and expense claims.

Maybe she's waiting
for her lover to leave his wife?
Hope weighted
by the disappointment to come.

I stand to leave.
As I scatter coins
into the saucer
she turns towards me,
drops the mask
and allows her eyes to smile.
The day lifts.

Web Weaving

In our mid morning hotel room
slatted blinds slice sunlight into dark
lines bar-coding your naked body.
On the floor lies a chaos of clothes,
the discarded skins of every-day life
entwined, as we were,
in those incandescent moments.

Time is slowing now, it can be counted
in the float of dust motes
that voyage across my eyes
as they imbibe your presence.

I think of the deceits and tears
that have led us here.
Then, as it always does,
comes the rising cumulus of guilt.

I feel I'm trapped in a dark forest
where ivy embraces oak
in slow loving strangulation.

You smile at my dilemma
and beckon me across the room.
I step out of the shadows,
lost, once more, in your light.

Can Stones Ever Love

On the shore waves inhale,
water threads its weave
around tide worn rocks;
I place my hands on hard granite.
It's cold, yet slick and sensuous.
Has this stone ever felt
the warmth of human skin,
experienced a caress?

Later, in a cottage on the headland,
cocooned in the *sloe black night*,
we explore deeper waters;
and in the uncertainty of our first kiss
the granite in me cracks.

The Punishment Of Lust
(painting in oils by Giovanni Segantini 1891)

Conjoined souls of phantom women
poise over iced earth;
sisters, half forming;
floating in, floating out.
I imagine their breath, in hiding,
thin, lost.

Pigment, oil and a thousand cuts
of brush-stroke
paint new meaning into old words.

Are they the dead and dying,
or the now and becoming?
It makes you think.
It makes me think
of lips pressed against lips;
your breath, my breath.

It makes me think of afterwards,
watching you sleep.
Your long hair inking pillows,
sketching the night.
The slow rise and fall
of your breasts,
soft curve of stomach
and that moment when we were one breath.

I stand before a painting.
I stand next to you,
we're standing together before a painting,
kissing:
trying to make sense of it all.

Migrating The Soul

Too young to be a snowbird
he still flew south,
away from winter's claw
away from memory.

On a beach at the end of the Keys
he discovered a shell,
its spirals infinitely curving.
He carried it with him constantly
believing in its uniqueness.

Then he found her-
or so she let him think.

At night they would lie together,
limbs woven close,
listening to the churn of waves
on forgotten shells:
secure in the heavy heat
of skin touching skin.

And for a time there was no winter.

Changing Seasons

On a mid March morning
a surrender of white laundered sheets
smack against freshly painted sky.
A pair of blackbirds scout
the borders seeking softer bedding.

She stands at the back door,
carbolic cracked hands
wringing a tea towel;
watches the birds jitter
at moss and twig, senses
their bond, envies their love.

Back in the empty nest
she places the last of his clothes
in a jumble-sale bag, pausing
only to touch the fading bruise
that still yellows her cheek.

She returns to the washing;
blackbirds have left
their calling card;
it stains the starched cloth.
She smiles then laughs,
because this will no longer
be *her* fault.
The long winter of him
has finally gone.

Bumping Into Doors

The view used to be rose coloured
with washes of warm amber;
back then he saw only what he wanted,
now everything's a miasma of mottled purple.

This is the window of his soul,
multi-hued, constantly chameleon,
and each day he sees the world's facets
through a new pane.

Recently he's been on the outside
looking in, a voyeur to his own thoughts.
But the vistas have become opaque,
only seen through watered-down milky
cataracts of self-doubt.

He thinks he sees her
standing at the kitchen table
kneading dough; fluid feminine
hands relishing the soft elasticity.

When the mist dissipates
he sees she is gouging
at a face that was once his.
So empowered.
So strong.
She's no longer bumping into doors.

The End Of The Pier

Salt cracked decking is aged silver,
loose change drawn to the penny arcade,
only the policeman no longer laughs
out loud at what the butler saw.

Wind drives endless spiteful seas
that suck and gnaw at the arthritic
old man bones of corroded girders,
joints swollen under a crusting of barnacle.

An Empire believed you would stand
forever, providing respite from factory
and farm. Britannia ruling the waves
all for a nominal entrance fee.

Tearstains of rust run like mascara
after a broken romance, they soil the once
white fascias of this fractured finger
that points from a troubled shore.

I turn towards you; notice you're reading
a faded poster announcing that by popular
demand 'The Good Old Days'
are returning, matinee half price.

You believe it less than I do. The café
where tea is served tan and thick beckons.
we walk absently apart, your mascara
begins to run; it must be the wind.

The Other Side Of The Sky

Every morning she combs the beach
in the company of her dogs;
she loves her dogs.

She scans the horizon
searching for phantom ships,
hoping they'll crash to the shore,
broken sparred, spilling a treasure of verse.
But all she ever gleans are shards
of words, which she hoards
until she transcribes them
in the end terrace she calls home.

Back in the bitter lemon twist
of memory there was once a man
and a son she chooses not to know.

She has all she needs,
sand, the blank canvas of sky
and weight of fountain-pen,
the familiar conduit between thought
and page. When birthing is done
and infant letters still bear
the damp cowl of India ink, the paper
is placed in a dark cupboard
to suffer the jaundice of self doubt.

Neighbours no longer call.
The word *friend* was never
in her lexicon. She has her beach,
her words and her dogs;
she loves her dogs:
all of them, except the black one
that constantly claws
from the other side of the sky.

An Elephant In The Bloom

It's unseasonably warm,
we're sitting in your garden
and I've brought you red roses.

You ask how I've been;
Good. And you?
Good.

My cellophane clothed
statement of intent,
lies unnoticed on the table.

If you were to take them inside,
trim stalks, seal sap
in boiled water

and arrange them in a vase
it would be a sign.
They remain unmoved.

Over weak tea we prune
at the past, seeking meanings
to words behind words.

At some point,
during this desperate banality,
I notice a petal fall

and another and another
revealing the thorned stems
of what we really want to say.

I'll Call You

Your number's in the old diary,
the one I could never quite discard.
I resolve to phone,

I don't. The week progresses
to its usual rhythm
of work, television and tedium.

Wednesday, I've destroyed the diary
but your number refuses to leave.
It's started to play tricks.

Two raindrops on a petal,
I sneeze five times, eat one apple,
count three magpies and four slugs.

Dreams come, your lips brushing mine:
on the cusp of a caress
you breathe numbers into my mouth,

and in the weakness of dawn
I reach for the phone. The battery's dead,
maybe it's an omen.

Not eating today, I'm leafing the paper.
The number becomes a mantra
intoned until it's rendered meaningless;

that was the plan; inevitably
my finger stutters on the dial pad.
You don't answer. Your lover does.

Taking A Moment

Snow-melt leaches from fell tops.
Windermere, as deep as longing,
mirrors March sky and ripples
with each dip of swan's beak.

Sound plays charades,
hides in sudden corners,
waits to ambush ears
with a chirring of gull wings,
or plaintive chime of hillside sheep.

A couple stands at the end of the jetty
not waiting for the ferry.
Movement is not needed to travel
on this day of possibilities.

Fireworks In The Park

On a late September night
we recline on pillows of crisp
amber horse chestnut leaves.
Above us seams of silver and gold
explode through the dark ore of sky.

Pungent smoke etches
the chill air as we gasp
and laugh at each new detonation.
We may be approaching autumn
but tonight we embrace
childhood wonder of spring.

We Do Like...

On this nothing day
sheets of gunmetal cloud migrate landward
and the beach dons an ochre overcoat.

A solitary sandcastle erodes
its salt burdened windmill tilting
under the weight of indifference.

Donkeys huddle, brine crusted hair
hanging in snags. A million miles away
the reluctant tide sulks ashore.

On the promenade a beige macked couple sit in silence
eking out thermos and crab paste sandwiches.
Only three hours left before the coach departs.

Patients

We were whole,
now we are not.
Scalpel's slice has altered our terrain,
hands have delved.

We lie on our beds,
diminished,
defined by wire and tube.

Days are measured by the turn
of tea trolley wheel, heat of needle
and slow drop of drip.

We know new words,
some only whispered
during the dark hours:
some become placebos of hope,
'Prognosis, possibility , probability.'

We used to be us,
now we're an entity;
we are Ward Fifteen B.

Remembrance

'Where's my son, where's he gone?
You're old, you're not my Michael.'

Always the same litany;
confusion looped in repetition,
recited in the day room, it echoes
off flaking walls, seeps into soiled carpets,
joins the broken-biscuit smell of decay.

'Have you finished your homework?
You'll feel the strap if you haven't,
who are you anyway?'

She searches for connections,
emits fractured lighthouse beams
of lucidity; tries to guide memories
home. Normal service will not resume.

'Watch out for your little sister.
Mind you cross on the Zebra.'

Her regression reinforces his guilt;
hones constant visions of scattered
schoolbooks, broken pencils and crimson
stained gingham. He wishes he could
change places with mother.

Eavesdropping

Perched on high-wire phone lines,
starlings Morse-code the air
with incessant chatter.
Beneath their talons cables, vibrate
to a mélange of human voices.

She's at it again... can't get the stain...
only three days remain... I'll have a number four
with extra rice... if only he wasn't so nice...
I won't tell you twice...

Each conversation
spirals down copper ley lines
feeding the birds' hunger;
laughter, sadness, banality beyond belief;
they're not fussy eaters.

They soar,
a tower of Babel
inking the air,
ruby sun cloaked by the swarm.
The starlings roost –
their dreams man-made.

Switching The Electric Ventilator Fan Off

It lurks on the kitchen worktop
a throwback encased in nicotined
Bakelite, propeller blades caged
behind rusted metal,
plug crusted with cockroach tracks.

At some point it became ambitious,
no longer content to graze stale air,
fragments of conversation
began to disappear. Occupants
of the apartment were left
with sentences hanging in mid-air.
Absence of explanations led to murder.

Detectives were puzzled by the lack
of blood – they failed to notice
small red globules oozing
from the frayed flex.

I'm the latest tenant.
I've learnt not to waste words.
If the silence becomes too much
I lean towards the constant chattering
blades hoping to catch a regurgitated
phrase. I know things I shouldn't.

It's started to extract my thoughts.
I can't think how to turn it off.
On on on.
I think... I meant... on?

On The Face Of It

We all live on the other side of our appearances. Our Faces belong
more to others than they do to us.
Anthony Gormley, Sunday Times 29/10/06

They hang in the hallway
like sallow skinned Dali Watches
but with eyes, noses and lips.
A face for every occasion,
some smile, some scowl sullenly;
the most menacing remain impassive
silently anticipating selection.

His requirements are many,
he strives to achieve
that certain
look.

He was observed leaving the scene,
only no one could agree
who he was. I suspect
he had a couple of spares
concealed within the folds
of his gabardine raincoat.

No charges were ever brought.

Looking Skywards Down

Come with me, float up stream to a land
where the taste of colour runs strong on the tongue,
the sight of sound seduces the eye
and songs fragment into rainbows.
A land where blue buttercups cavort,
dancing free over strawberry hued fields.

A land where trees have persuaded bees
to build sparkling starling-feathered nests;
places for twiggy babies to warble
their woody tunes. A land where fish
tumble through a tide of streets
pecking playfully at geraniums
that hang from top hat planters.

Visit shops that sell raccoon dusted duvets,
pink peppers and sergeants stripes.
See the baker's wife knead dragon fire
into honey roasted loaves. Watch the penny
round policeman wobble after robbers
who've stolen a pound of fresh air;
he never catches them as they always
exhale before he can get near.

On the corner of Walrus Lane Miss Lucy
hovers high in the sky dressed only in echoes;
a brace of cats entwined in her hair.
She dispenses words of wisdom but only
to those who will not hear.

And if you follow the signposts
that tell you where you've been
eventually you'll come to the village green
and witness Anteaters dance around a maypole
made from faeries' unfinished thoughts.

But now, as the sun rises in the west,
our trip has run its course and we must
take our leave. So where have we been?
Well, actually nowhere; unless you truly believe.

Clearing The Air

I'm out on the marsh,
that thin ribbon of almost land
and constantly chameleon
excess of sky;

my only company
a stalking heron
moving in angles,
jagging here and there
on impossible legs.
I share its awkwardness.

Then it flies,
parson grey wings
possessing thermals.

Its dagger beak snags
a wisp of cloud,
drags it landward
over the slow pulse
of radiated heat.

Cumulus froths
form fractal edges,
become engorged
until it can hold back
no more.

Ozone rips as the first
unsalted teardrops fall.
Steel taste of electricity
sloughs across my tongue
as thunder wrenches heavens canvas.
Lightening neon's shapes
a horse's mane, an inverted castle
and the ever present abyss.

Then it's gone,
heading eastward
as all things do.

The heron returns
seeking something more substantial
than mist.
From its slow dot of eye
tacit understanding
ripples outwards.
I take note,
walk onwards, as I always do.

Roger McGough's Socks

A trainee poet, of no fixed ability,
seeking inspiration, quaffed the night away.
Awakening at dawn, semi naked on the lawn,
he perceived a figure emerging from the mist.
It was Saint Roger McGough,
wearing a Balinese skirt, Scottish Dirk
and oddly florescent socks.

Trainee poet awestruck by this visionary
'Pontiff Of Pun' begged and pleaded
to be blessed with what he needed;
awaywithwords.
He grovelled, he groaned, he moaned platitudes
by the dozen. Saint Roger, shell-shocked
from this cannonade of clichés, produced
his latest collection, withdrew a concrete poem
and promptly dropped it on the trainees foot.

It was all very messy.

Syllables cymballed across the grass
crashing into phrases which fractured
and fractalled away. An entire sentence
ricocheted of the shed downing a passing
Pigeon. Then in a haze of imagery
Saint Roger was gone.

Trainee poet was admitted to hospital.
His body having been immersed in verse
now sprouted sonnets, rondels and rhyme;
a condition that could only be alleviated
by severe editing. Couplets were carved
from his spine, the spleen yielded an entire stanza,
whilst commas littered his lungs.

The trainee wrote no more; but often, when ginned,
he would mutter about the poetry he felt within.

A Wasps Nest

My kitchen cupboards are spotless;
row after row of hand polished tins
neatly stacked against boxes of bitterness,
sachets of jealously and jars of vitriol.
I've checked their sell by dates
and you'll be glad to know
they're good for many years yet.

Now it's time to inspect the bathroom;
cleanliness is next to godliness.
Next to him, next to her, next to *them*
I am truly sanitary. My sanctuary
is replete with fragrance, soothing oils
and prejudice. There's nothing like a good
soak in some misinformed bigotry.

By the time I sink to my cellar
I'll be happily deluded by the tabloid
wallpaper that covers the cracks
of my white, white, white washed
myopic walls. Yes you can see that
my life is clean and that I am always
right. Very, very, very right.

Curtain Call

He greasepaints over broken
capillaries and liver spotted skin
that was always too thin to rebut
the ink of a critic's pen.

He's third ugly sister
in a second rate seaside resort
that should have been shut down
along with the railways.

Each evening a boredom of parents
bring their offspring to cheer and jeer.
They hardly hear his slurred
lines as they bay, *it's behind you;*

he doesn't need to be reminded.

Taking Your Time

Time
is
no
thing,
the never ending ocean;
its waves swathing
the illusion of reality.
It becomes and unbecomes.
Time
just
is.

Now and then exist
in the beat of a hummingbird's wing.
Yet we reduce time to symbols,
imprison it behind glass,
make it walk the treadmill
of seconds, minutes and hours.

If we could set time free
from its linear life
I wouldn't have to say
I'll love you forever,
I could just love you now.

To Be Continued

Memory unravels:
aroma of grandmother's chicken broth,
the brittleness of October
and low chatter of train tracks.
The cadence of laughter,
whir of crematorium curtains
or fingers touching frosted grass.

These are some of the words
that shape my secret poem.
I've been writing it for years,
stanzas softly gripping my heart
as my mouth stays silent.

At times nothing is written,
fallow days ebb into weeks,
weight of words heavy
against the granite of a full stop.

Then there are times of plenty,
a surfeit of images thundering,
cascading, colliding,
building and demolishing towers of Babel.

My latest acquisition is a crimson butterfly,
it nestles in a synapse between a shark's tooth;
and an echo of school dinners.
It seems happy, waiting to take its place
in the unending parade.

I spin endless lines, cut and spin again.
No place to begin, no place to end;
strength comes from silence,
what remains unsaid cannot be wrong.

Indigo Dreams Publishing
132, Hinckley Road
Stoney Stanton
Leicestershire
LE9 4LN
www.indigodreams.co.uk